# About the Author

Teresa Doughty was born in Scotland in 1947 and she was always caught up in the world of imagination, expressing it visually and with words. She is a graduate of The Open University.

Her career as a painter was not wide ranging but the wellsprings were deep. She then took up the themes in her work as an artist and produced a body of writing , expressing her feeling for the landscape of Scotland, and her rich life's experience.

# Dedication

This book is dedicated to Moyra, Ann, Jon, and Marcia, dear companions on life's journey.

Teresa Doughty

# MY GREAT BRAVE TUNES

## A COLLECTION OF POEMS

AUSTIN MACAULEY
PUBLISHERS LTD.

A CIP catalogue record for this title is available from the British Library.


ISBN 9781785540905 (Paperback)
ISBN 9781785540912 (Hardback)


www.austinmacauley.com

First Published (2015)
Austin Macauley Publishers Ltd.
25 Canada Square
Canary Wharf
London
E14 5LQ




Printed and bound in Great Britain

# Poems of Land and Sea

Glencoe 1

From Rannoch Moor
coming into Glencoe
the curtain of mist draws back
to reveal the grand drama of Glencoe
the awesome presence –
height upon height of rock piles
drifting in and out of veils of torn rainclouds
now entering the land of the other world...

## Deep Waters

And on the boat to Knoydart –
still sea like black silk
hardly a ripple or motion
the wake of the water is white lace.

The Sea is Woman
all dressed to kill.

## Coming up to Crianlarich 1

The quiet earth
breathes like a woman
the soft leaves and grass; like maidenhair,
bracken gold brown.
Look at it, look at it
look once and forever.
Dappled shapes of shadowed leaves,
the sheep, the earth, the trees
sing for the branches of green swinging, going up to Mallaig
once more.
Once again we'll see,
chantilly lace of birches, heather,
all purple, and silver,
the luxuries of autumn
and oh – the sea
did I forget?
Oh – the sea, the sea.

## Paint the Mountain

Quaint – aincha, aincha –
like ice-cream cones turned upside-down
and the flood water pouring down,
melt water,
and white peaks engaging with the ragged clouds greyer than
the snow.
Icy water in the burns, torrents in full spate
creamy water swirls among the trees
silver birches pulled and drowned.
Wet spring, no greens yet.
Brown bracken, browner depths spills,
the white waters ruffled, tumbling
this chilly March morning.
Bleak lands.

## Arisaig, 1955

The smell in the air of the blaeberries
rosy breath of the sun on a rock
crisp heather and salt-kissed grass
sea-tossed wrack foaming between rock clefts
scattered sun dazzle glittering on the stream
soft white sand, a myriad grains
sifted through the hourglass of eternity,
all nature's creatures rocking in the passion of the waves
surely, Lord, the blessed land...

## Jewel

It's in the spaces in between
that you find the jewel of time
words cannot count
the spaces in between the beads

strung on the gossamer of destiny
forever, never….flies time
and once again we count
forgetting – it's in the spaces in between...

## The Field of Dreams, Back of Keppoch

On the beaches, in the rocks
the secrets of my heart are locked
the phrases of divine expression
will not go away or lessen
in the schists of Arisaig
in the seaweeds on the bay
in the rustling of the waves,
are mantras of my understanding.
In the breath of skies and mists
no false witness will exist
but the fields are full of tares, just as we are full of cares.
Is it ever as it seems, in the field of dreams?

Listen to the Wind

Passion, the river of life;
listen to the wind
and the song of the sea.
So little time to go
so little time to be.
Let's dance barefoot in the rain,
we may not come here again,
feel the joy as well as pain.

I have no home, I dance among the stars
and I'll always be a wanderer.

## Evening

The blooming blossoming music
spills onto the night
and overflows Heaven's edges.
A drama of stars
yearns for music that treads softly in my dreams,
touch deftly wild strings in the dark.
No one knows where the wind blows
telling tales of the melodies in my heart.

## Glencoe ll

We came here once
through the snow
into Glencoe.

All frivolity ceases
as we view the savage grandeur of the peaks;
the haunted splendour
of stony cracks and wrinkled gullies,
black angled slabs, spiky trees

dark and heavy,
as the ghosts of past and present
are slipping through the grey rain.

## Convalescing, Recovery

I see the hacketty beauty
of the sunlit clouds
all damp and dragging over
the distant city flats and towers

a windup by unworldly powers
no doubt,
to throw me into beauty once again,

and – wondering why,
in the dilatory rain, I'm here,
and even hovering
one foot tense
and one foot left behind,
as I'm stepping into
the lovely rhythm of life again.

Oh – and I forgot the pain!
Will this explain?
Amen.

## Glencoe lll

As I look up at the speechless crags
oh Glencoe –
mean and moody, you keep your secrets
whatever the weather
sombre, un-sunlit, pale grass and heather
dumb battalions of rocks, in the icy waters -
and on to Rannoch.

## Coming up to Crianlarich II

Looking up into the high sierras
to the snow-dusted mountain tops,
the misty heights of nowhere;
it takes the breath away, surely.

No cleverness
no smarty-pants required here.

It's awesome.

I stand before you, God,
thanking you for this day
for another year
to wonder still, and wander
and be content.

## Pilgrimage

The grandeur of the hills takes me by surprise
the route to the west unfolds before my eyes
a pact with this land is in my soul
poetry fills it up like a golden bowl.
Glasgow to Mallaig wends its haunting way
champagne in my veins is no match for this day.

The railway uncurls along the valley-side
and gentle sun lights up the sloping hill
brown brackens left from last year's summer
and bud-bursting trees to celebrate Easter.
We're nobody's fool, we poets
folk always find their way home
to God's own country.

# Gold and Silver Words

## Silence is Golden, Speech is Silver

And in between lies the written word,
silent but powerful, silver communication
gold light of the sun, tears of the moon
saying all that needs to be said, creeping into our heads
from all the dreamtimes
the pen mightier than the sword
ideas could change destiny at a word
the sword of the mind, and deeds of the day
all from inner being change the world
the ripple on the ocean, or the footsteps of a mouse
move time forward in ways un-thought.
God's hand, unseen, works through the hearts of folk
straw spun to gold
transforming chaos, hurt , and pain
into subtle beauties, profoundly sweet
unlooked for moments we could miss
and mourn if we are not aware of this.
So grasp the life and shake it, wring the meaning out
before it slips into the long forgotten lake
expressed in silver tongue, how we can speak
and written down in silence, purest gold...
To my friends , et al...

## Raw

With the rawness of my anger
coming out of my eyes
I see my loving kindness
to my surprise.

Deep in my soul
the knife edge turns,
passion for loving
still in me burns.

Oh Lord of life
where are your answers?
I've burned my bridges and
I'll take no more commands.

# Notes on the Referendum for Scottish Independence

Grey, grey, the eyes of my country
looking inward, see grey cities and grey skies.
I count on a rain-wet pessimism,
that new autonomy of government denies
the words of conquering heroes
are converging, near enough these days
to merge the present with the past.
From Fionn McCoull to Burns to Donald Dewar
our leaders quote the songs of Scotland for their power
while drinkers weep sad pities in their beer.
So let all us Scots be of good cheer.
The 'Flower of Scotland' has not happened yet
the future's just a seed in growth
to nurture with a vote for 'yea' or 'nay'
The Stone of Scone is in its place again
let's will Scottish independence in
and throw worn pessimism away.

## At St. Andrews Cathedral, October

The golden leaves are blowing here;
nature's detritus on the autumn street.
There's hesitancy in the space
that soars
that moment, is that moment in the street
and so too, do the gravestones speak
above the racket of the chattering world.
The dead shout louder in their silent peace
than many fizzing furies of our current times.
The sense they say is lost to us,
we don't connect, we're in the dark –
more than the dead, the dear departed
that sing the song of life
which we don't hear….
I'll pray we could be listening now.

## Cinderella

In between the doing and the thinking
do I care if you loved me?

I see where sunlight falls palely
on crumbs on the messy table –
and I'm hesitating –
such poignant minutes fill the silences.

Lentils and ashes in the fireplace
meatbones and scraps on the dishes
Cinderella can sort the mundane
but she's lost with the profound

and wondering, yes, going deeper.
Did you love me ?
Yes, yes, you did. The glass slipper.
No worries.

## Some Reflections on Riots, Unrest, Homelessness, and People in Dire Straits

In some major dramas of life
secrecy hides betrayal
hidden pain in silence
consumer driven culture
swallows the human story.

'Reality TV' enacts tales of trivia
like a figment of mass imagination –
the latest enthralling soap series

and homeless people, the disempowered
the luckless, the unloved
are truly dramatic
unknown, unrealised
sleeping in the doorways of the metropolis.

Their misery; a payment for sins –
and blind to its selfish motives
society is seeking 'culture,' 'drama'
and spitting in the face of humanity.

## Lost Love, 4am

It is quiet now. The day breaks
and red steals softly through the sky.
Relentlessly my body aches;
the depths are touched by thunders of love.
My world is shaken with tears that move.
I was not there when you went by.

About Death

All promises of Heaven
would not tempt me from the beautiful Earth.
No God could offer so profound a beauty
as Gaia, the lover and beginning of my birth
paradise I find a little bitty short of wonder
in my small span of time.
So I will not rush towards my end
to leave my poor body like a broken leaf,
dropped down and forgotten
for it served me well.

## Acknowledgement

When greening comes in May
I do remember
at apple blossom time I recognize you
I never did acknowledge all my feelings.
It was as if my blindness was intent.

The tears come as I hear the birds sing
some poignant hours with you I'd spent
my lover, you are sweetly on my mind now
so, sadly, do I wish you well my friend.

I don't know what I'm struggling to express
but, a warmth and yearning
a burning tenderness

You rocked my world, and then away forever
you made a sweetness, and then were quietly gone
leaving an imprint on my mind.

It's unmistaken, a mark on time
my air had changed, with you beside me.


My heart is torn, in early May
each sunrise, love steals softly through
my dreams,
my memories, of you.
You touched my arms, my heart
then disappeared
leaving a tremor on the air.
I wonder where you are my dear....

And still the birds sing every May
at the breaking of the day
almost there, I cannot say
nor forget, nor forget...

## Mortality

The song behind it
a veil between now and the hereafter
is very thin.

It echoes, echoes, but I cannot enter in.

Please God endure for me,
the depths in which I sin

for I am a butterfly
underneath a pin.

## The Ancient Hippie

Yes, it's lovely to be old,
there are moments of pure gold
when looking back to times of discord,
confusion reigned or life was hard.

Resolved, the pieces fall in place
in such a crystal perfect shape,
amazed, astonished - peaceful grace
has taken over what was broke
and somehow fashioned a perfection
giving here a new direction
for valued kindness and affection.

Brown Hair

Oh woman of mystery
with your long brown hair
plucking sparkles out of the air
save it's a face that may not be there
shimmer of passions
seen through a veil
and an eye that stares
through forms of flowers imagined in space
though who knows where...

## A Poem for Toni

'Women and children first'
is the theme of inconspicuous gallantry
when both are the priority
of a woman whom nobody knows.
No one has heard of her, save
in artwork, etching and prints.
She threads beauty through
her work and life
to create a new world
for the woman and child
forever loved.

## Virtue

I'll try not
to die, not
enshrouded in virtue
too likely then
it might be
my spiky self - the height of cheek
will take leave of
the notion of virtue.

# The Undiscovered Country

## The Alchemist

I wish I could sing
but failing that
like a dumb animal in silent torment
I create beautiful things
joy transcending the greyness of life
transfixed in metal
hills and sky, colour and light
transfigured, the pain of humanness
leads towards salvation.

## Grandpa's Garden

The echoes flee as fast as clouds
far away like blown out shrouds
like daffodils on Windyridge Hill.
The memories are with me still
In Grandpa's garden in the wind.
The windmills and the flying swing.
He pushed his girlie up so high
in the blue air, a lovely sigh.
Swing and daffodils in the sun
my Grandpa dear, in his autumn
but memories are always spring
of me and Grandpa and the swing.

## Velvet

Honeyed strings of Persian delight
singing of the fire in my belly.
No tomorrows please,
let me stay here for a space.
The sweetness of a lover
lying in the dawn like a dozing animal
soft skin and hair,
sleep on him.
Away in dreams, dream on lover
may you rock in the bosom of night
till dawn breaks...

## Milano Duomo

I hear a hollow beating in the vault above my head,
the murmur of a million pigeons' wings
echoing in the roof of God's house.
A throbbing pulse is hidden among the pointed gothic spires
the stained glass saints' voices, crystal clear with age
intermingle in the hanging draperies of bishops' tombs.
A faint smell of dry stone, and the dim gold twilight of the church
shines with rich colours on the dark high pews.
High in the dome, stone saints and doves are talking unknown things
through the still sounding air
far above the tap of heels on the mosaic marble floor.

Christmas Thoughts

Softly sad, the snow lies on the platform.
The train pulls out ablaze with lights
and commuters are all quite warm inside.

The snow falls soft,
its whirling mystery so quiet, silent, and profound.

The season's come, of Christmas.
Deepest winter
and all the plants lie sleeping in the earth.

The angels' voices now are heard above us
in thin and subtle tunes –
I strain to hear.

They are singing out and telling us
and calling
of the everlasting wonder of Christ's birth.

## Mont Cenis Pass

It is wild, it is mad
under the stars at Mont Cenis.
Half a gale is blowing
in the windy heights
miles above anywhere,
the tops of the Alps rise towering above
with snow in the hollows.
The grass is wet, and covered with Alpine flowers underfoot.
Up, and yet up, high above
hangs a sliver of moon
like an icicle in the cold crisp clear sky
shining with bright white light.
And suddenly I shiver,
small and insignificant
in the windy pasture
cold, with the hugeness of the sky meeting the Alps
cold and insignificant,
in the blackness of the night...

## Flawed
*For Angus*

And I am swept up in beauty
as the tips of the tall pines
connect with the airbrushed clouds
and soft light creeps through the wet pale sky
tentative, it's on the edge, the beauty
as our humanness is – frail, imperfect, flawed
so heart catching
the tears come.

## Reflection on a Washed Up Tree at Balmerino

Huge, heavy, deep and profound
the washed up tree on the beach at Balmerino
above the tideline, stranded, desolate, a skeleton
unthinking, the mainstream of the tide
the Tay hastens to the estuary
leaving this monolithic anachronism
like a beached whale
dying, life ebbing, abandoned, forgotten –
as if I were a great anachronism
my artwork is stranded above the tideline
my life is out of step with the mainstream
the spring tides may be too late for me –
'gifts of the spirit', needed but not required.

## On the Purity of Candlelight

The strange beauty of the lapping light
carries on echoes into the night.
My soul carries itself on the waves.
Echoes of light fly into the eaves.
Never will I to this earth return,
unto the next land I will yearn,
gone further than the flesh I will burn.

## Love

Love is a dream that fades like withered leaves.
This last one is quivering on the twig, not wanting to go
but the relentless cold wind snatches it from its frail hold
and sweeps it away with the rest.
No memoriam for dead leaves.
No memoriam for dead loves.

## Sudden Summer Rain

Pom pom pompadour roses
bouncing under heavy rain
knifey slicing cuts of rain
sheeting down from a dark sky
wizard wind from cracks in the clouds
creeps beneath the branches
soughing out the spirit of the place
roses gleaming, soft and pink
glowing, dripping , fragrant
dance about as if to music, in the slashing rain...

Autostrada

Andante
buon giorno
say the bells – a carillon of campaniles
Florence in the morning
Tutti – what like it? Only
Buonissimo, the eternal music
of Italian speech, strange and exciting as the Italian Lakes
lost in a cool amethyst haze
a shifting dazzle of spectral reflections
slanting slopes of sun off blasted slabs
dust, dust, and more dust
swirls up like dervishes from the roads.
Ecco, ragazza, under Coca-Cola umbrella
parched music of the Autostrada
Ants andante;
an adventure, a migration of the populace
timestricken, strada, strada
Autostrada…

Flowers in the Car Park

By the damp and pungent purple of the buddleias
rain is drizzling among the greens
and smudgy scattered shadows
softly shine among the blossoms.

Inside, outside – the double negative
shine on, iridescent flowers.

The car park is lit up.

# All My Great Brave Tunes

## Valedictory

The strange beauty of a loving touch
cannot be stretched beyond the power in my heart.
The strength of caring could be such
as all the 'anam caras' in my mind were great brave tunes
and thus my dear I prayerfully think of you
and hesitate before the gates of death.
Your loving touch anticipates the outgoing of my breath.

Caught in the urgent pools of your eyes,
I catch my breath with surprise;
no I was not here before
I cannot for my life deny my want of you,
your young and vital light
eclipses my fears and inevitable death,
a swansong for my ever loving end.

## Spooked Woman

She is running barefoot through the corridors
stone beneath her feet
cool and grey
mellow, mellow mists roll in
half a hundred passed – years,
while I watch and wait.
The crashing chords take note of time passing
whither away lady? To catch the last trip to love.

## Tantra evening

And all my 'anam caras' would be great brave tunes
One hundred times I'd play these tunes anew
so softly now in evening light my dear
my Jon, now knowing you it all comes clear
the singing water softly soothes my heart
and runs between us like the moons of love
my trembling soul was filled with such delight
surprised, you seemed, by my unravelled self
at peace and wishing for your kiss and touch
my friend, my dear, would you be such
that I could trust in 'love' once more?

## Flower Song

One day when I was walking along
my heart flipped over and stopped still
with silken eyes my lover gazed at my soul;
a flower in the desert
a song in the dust
water from an oasis, silken waves of hair like to the sea
of all the great brave tunes – my' anam caras'
my great brave song.
Song of the desert, canzonetti
like to them was never heard
songs of rain in the wilderness
slipping into my heart
oh in between the sheets
with softness touching you touching me
oh all my great brave tunes
a tender flower song.

## To my Lover, Over the Hills and Faraway

An ecstasy of wonder gripped my soul
when I saw you lying on the couch asleep
like a child so innocent and soft
in beauty so may all the angels keep.

I wonder where you journeyed at that time.
Your soul was roving on in bliss and peace
unconscious, lovely, so relaxed , you're mine
one hand lay dropped, in all the grace unknown.

*Would not wake you ever, still it seems*
*you were so happy lost in dreams*
*a moment caught in time was crystallized*
*eternity sits always by our side.*

For My Toyboy

As I slipped out of sight, 'away weary, away,'
not happy, hoping for any more for me!
That freshens up to sharp, as we reach the level
and always present, the perfection of oases in the raw
the lovely nude, you see.

Male beauty stops the breath in gasps.
Their clever side was never in the frame
the lovely, glistening hair and skin stops short
of dragon's teeth sowed in the graceful game.

And with the key to life dropped in my hand.
I turn with surprise from out this land
I 'was not was' - a woman's only one
I've gratitude to have been here at this time.

Heartbreak Hotel

And all our yesterdays lit up my life, dear Jon
my memory is full of loveliness
the present is with you in mind, my dear
for us there's no tomorrows hand in hand.

The time we had, so I recall, was grand.

Oh Jon, Oh Jon,
I see you sitting in my chair
or on my sofa, naked, bare
your hands all messing through my hair
your presence, man, is everywhere.

My tears fall fast and hot and wet
I see you in my mind and yet
elusive circumstances say
you won't be mine, they say me nay
your precious soul I'm mindful of
as ran between us moons of love
no other man loved me so well
I'm here for now in Heartbreak Hotel.

The Lorelei

Walk tall, away from me then
'No regrets,' you'll say
'she was nice, huh,
I broke her bloody heart.'
Oh sir you did not tread softly with me
and I am the fairy that will infiltrate your dreams...
I am the Lorelei.

## Goodbye , Gypsy Jon

Do a deal with me, Rainbow Chameleon
you go your way and I'll go mine
but wherever you go – shine, shine, shine.

I'd turn the divine into the vernacular
and the vernacular into the divine
…you were always on my mind.

You are the thief of time, gypsy Jon
so go your ways, your roads
and wherever you go – shine , shine
but Big Jon, Big Fella, in my heart – you're mine.

# Some Lunar Poems

## All the Rest

I would like to rest
in the shadow of your smile.
I would like to go along the road a bit
and lean on your arm
for the last mile
or so

for a little while
and take the time
to hear the music of the years
tumble past my ears.

I would like to rest for a space
with the kindness in your face
and a little gentleness would not be out of place.

A song for living might be seemly here
I've gratitude
for a loving touch
and thoughts of grace…

## To My Lover

There is a silence where you were.
My hair stands up like brittle grasses
if ever I think but that you're dear
or forget how much time passes.
The cold of loneliness embraces
all memories in time
but you were spoken for, in truth
you were not mine.

## Rainbow Cat

Not only, but also – I
will rest in the shadow of your smile
oh yes, oh my, my kitty friend,
I'll name you - 'not only but also'
because you came in beneath my sigh
when I'd felt that I could die.
In joy and play one summer day
to chase the blues away, and say –
it is - 'not only but also – the laughing and the tears,
it is not always pain
the love will come again, the dark won't be forever
rainbows form with sun and rain.'
Not only but also, my rainbow friend…my catty…

## The Lintie

Listen to the Lintie sing
in dark places music rings
perched on the godforsaken edge of Hell
the music bird's voice, it's there
fluttering, the gold harp's tunes
chasing grace notes like a bell.

Warmed, the heart is whole again
enclosing darkness, troubles, pain.
Once more the sun breaks through
and music chases clouds away

an end to all the gloom and fear
suddenly it seems no cross to bear
because on the edge where we despair
that joyful bird, the lintie, sings.

Testament

As I walk through the park
all dressed in black
my skirt blowing
in my widow woman weeds
my red hair flying like a flag.

At dusk, along the paths
in the park, among the trees
my heart bleeds, bleeds –
I feel I'm on my knees.
No way do I live here any more
I go, to where I come from
to where I belong.
Touched once more, a passionate breeze
soughs through my hair
as memories
without compare.
The worlds open, the sky lifts
I will go free
the tie between us, the bond, the cords of love;
I will cut free.
It was tender between you and me.

## The Evening Star

Ah, there she lies
like one solitary pure lily
like a blossom she glows – in the soft deep dark purple
the velvet night spreads out around her
she is the centre, the evening star.
Entranced, I gaze…
I am compelled by some great strong emotion
I lift her up, soft velvet falls about my hands.
Her beauty glows upon my face
her wide eyes smile…
She vanishes away.

## Snow

The eerie hush with snow fallen
as if all the world is waiting,
all the world is silent, praying.

This searing light of sun on snow,
the brilliant winter sun reflected
crisp icicles, shining rime

the smell so fresh and clear, of snow
clean and white, a wet smell
penetrating, dazzles the brain

and the crunch underfoot
as you gasp with cold
and venture out, wrapped
into the white wilderness…

## No Cash from Art

I walked away with a hollow frown
from the edges where the sun went down

too canny I was, through the ends of the means
to see gold stars come of my dreams
too damn dumbstruck.

## Lust Poem

My body aches with want.
It shakes me to the core,
arouses like a tidal wave,
passion, love, and more.

The brooding need that's in us
with heavy strength explodes
taking us together, into
where our comfort knows.

## Shining Pearls

All night long
the sonorous dark
steals up like velvet on my eyes.
Only the ticking clock
divides the minutes from themselves
so I'm looking, looking – oh
into the spaces in between.
The secret is
like a jewel of great worth
stitched to the inside – it's the truth
of our garment of life so lightly worn
but, cast away – the jewels are not lost;
they make a crown in Heaven above
'cos tears are shining pearls at last
adorning us when we learn how to love.

For all the 'anam caras'

Easy come, easy go
no burden placed upon friends,
they are the jewels in my heart.

Our paths go along together for a space
touching in peace
touching peace

along the paths of the world
did I imagine…or did we connect?

Some time ago
I saw in my dreams
the shape of things
and all the ghosts apparent,
my long lost friend…..

## The Gift

As I sit here in the silence
almost a lifetime ago
my son and I, had a bond
what was that, so long ago?
Never a call - 'how are you , Mum?'
It's all washed away…
As I sat there, a lifetime ago,
I was – the same, with a gift in my hands
for this harsh world
a golden thing in my heart
a song that cannot be sung
for I have no voice
it is silence
silence.

## Canto Hondo

I sing no more
The Canto Hondo
the deep song
my mouth is stopped with dust
you stand in sinister glory
consumed with lust
for self and binding things
your head is crowned with pride
your feet are gory
awash with tears and blood
I tell the story –
so many years ago
so long ago it was….
And now I'm going
to where no man is
nor will be
through the glimmering garden
across the twilight bridge
to endless light, a safe haven.

Grit in the Spokes

The gritty, gritty – oh the broken minutes limp by. My eye.
I take myself along like busted tram
a trolley-car that feels like a sham.
The banal, the greyness, the zipped-up intentions
to past colour – not even honourable mentions….

Swing low – chantez le bas
the sweet chariot will carry you far
depending on how sincere you are.

Down on the grass hoodie craws are kinder it seems
than mechanical intent
grinding automatons sent
never more hellbent
than to get away with smashing the visions, and the dreams.

The hoodies, the craws, fly free in our world and theirs
only a few fly in the eye of the storm
and come to no harm, no harm.
Shalom.

# Potted Glory and Miscellanea

## Leaving My Home

This is a 'goodbye,' a tearing
a pulling away, what a grey feeling
shreds and tatters, blowing, whirling
dust, leaden ashes…
And after passion, love, there is no sharing
farewell to memories
I'm on my own, with me, myself, and I…
It is 'goodbye'

I cannot cry.

Potted Glory
*(For Tess and Liz O)*

Oh daring old women on the flying trapeze
we navigate the circadian skies with ease
our artworks are lovely, our adventures divine
we behave like teenagers and rebel all the time.

We travel the world to the antipodes
and push out the limits if faced with disease
we love with abandon, we're wounded with woe
we lived every minute, what a fine way to go.

Our secret of daring is ours if you please
we don't give a cuss, if brought to our knees
we wander on darkly, mostly tight-lipped
we know it's worth millions and so keep it zipped.

On a sermon by Judy White, 2012

The strength that is in weakness
gives pause –
a mystery this night
in silence a humility is plainly
coming in our sight.
Stepping out in quiet faith
and reaching out with trust
like children we are small and weak

but burned deep on the heart of God.

## Goodbye to Wur Pal, Never look Back

Gone without a wave –
a shout, a memory left, footsteps erased
no honour, it is, no mind –
the parting with my friend

our soldier man has gone, reneged
on a pal and comrade who
had been so close to him it hurt
and swiftly now, let down –
oh never mind!

Because it's only women, man,
you know – those things?
That torment us in our dreams
so should they, sir
happen they're people too
not honoured, not forgotten, so.

## Tie My Hair

And brown lie the rushes - o,
all dragged and ragged
like a maiden's hair
in the winter of life,
so caught and tenderly tied.
And greener grew the rushes – o,
and where do you bide,
my friend and lover, Jo?
Nor here nor there that I know
only in my heart I find.
Wildly and wantonly
you stride through every day
not heeding, nor seeing
where I was, it's so.
Tie my hair back tenderly
once again before I go.

## Wildflowers

I had written some poems about flowers, cultivated flowers that became wildflowers, that 'just growed, like Topsy', in their own sweet fashion, untended or pruned.

It would have been a lush, luxurious summer if it had been warmer, instead of chilly – one of the wettest. But the theme of wet blossoms permeated my mind in this year's brief season – plants adore the rain! And the natural world shines when suffused with water.

And there was a sweet sadness about it; about how we northerners long for the sun, so much that we don't appreciate the rain. Mists and mellow fruitfulness came early, but it was sweet, and the sadness perhaps a reflection of inner looking – raindrops seen as God's tears on the bursting peonies deep red, that I saw one day lately.

Life would not be savoured as profoundly happy if there was not sadness too. Nature can reflect the human condition and we are part of that expression, wildflowers symbolizing some nicer sentiments than the competition for survival that is part of it too.
Somehow the ruthless alienation of mankind's competitive civilization looks more unkind than nature's battles for survival. And that leads to anomie, soul sickness.

But wildflowers remind us of where beauty meets truth, and perhaps we need to rest in this beauty for a bit and put away our technologies - leave the rat race for a space. And be Pan's people, in the whispering shadows.

The Passing Years

So many years of unshed tears
are breaking through tonight
The Well at the World's End – is full of tears
it isn't right.

I see you walking by
with your brown hair softly blowing in the wind
the sunshine in your smile and a child in your arms

I burned and loved you once
I would not wish you harm
nor anything befall you untoward
I trust the angels guide your every step

and pray that in some other time we'll meet again
and walk together in the sunshine and the rain...

And all I have for you is flowers,
flowers, flowers in my hair...
Ave Maria.

At the Bottom of the Well

I'm in free fall, you betrayed me
lover, with your ruthless intent
impinged on my heart, as what you meant
to do, was unkind and cruel. I will vent
my fire on you some peaceful day.
And see if you can suffer, as you made me
to weep and ache for tenderness lost
they never were, the tarnished memories,
so precious, just what I'd felt.
You were so rapt in your intent
to score and graspingly consume
more than your need , at my expense.
My heart will break
you won't hear it crack
you're dull to others' pain
you lack
fellow feeling, love, respect.

I've hit the bottom, so I stand.

## Passages of Night

Listen to the rain patter
lilting down the long chords
for whom does the bell toll?
Echoing in the chambers of the night.

Where is my bluebird?
Enchanted evening, all alone
someday, maybe someday
I'll tell you how I feel for you.

Meanwhile in the corridors of dreams
I'll chant your name, my dear one
in harmony with the stars.

## Forget-Me-Not

My dear, in the farthest reaches of my mind
I found you – you were my kind
a golden thing was filled indeed
a touch of heaven blessed us both
the longing for the human touch
was found then lost, we could not stay
if it could be any other way…
Bear witness, don't forget, I pray.